I couldn't make it up
... if I tried!

By

Cornelia J. Glynn

Front cover design by Scott Gaunt scottgaunt@hotmail.co.uk

Image by: Cynoclub / Shutterstock.

Formatted by: PublishNation

Printed by: Lulu

Also by Cornelia J. Glynn:

The Power of Love –
A Transformational Guide to Living from the Heart

A Kindle e-book available from Amazon

Life is quite wonderful. Some things just happen, others we make happen. Whatever the occurrence, it can't be made up retrospectively. In this book I have chronicled twelve real life events that delight me even now.

The memory of my first encounter with a strange looking fruit called a *banana* still makes me smile and I still chuckle at a school friend's unusual advice on how to cure a common cold and the consequences when I followed it. Thinking of Truffles, an eccentric neighbour's potbellied pet pig, makes me laugh out loud. What about the time when a neighbour asked me to keep an eye on her car while she was away? I still feel foolish when she talks about it over coffee and on that note, if you were wondering where you can drink the ritziest brew ever, you will find the answer in this book…

Cornelia J. Glynn

In memory of Tina Jones

A FEW WORDS ABOUT ME

(Well, more than a few actually)

I was born, raised and educated in Germany and moved to London in my early twenties. I worked mostly in the music industry, although I aspired to become an Oscar-winning film producer. Well, some things aren't meant to be and the opportunity never arose. Instead I followed an innate desire to help others and explored the Healing Arts. I became a Diploma Homoeopath, a healer as well as practitioner and teacher of an ancient Hawaiian healing tradition.

Everything had been going quite well, when, aged 49 I suffered a brain haemorrhage and out-of-body experience. Within the space of less than a minute my life had changed beyond recognition. Having been a very active woman, I became so weak that even the minutest of tasks turned into a major undertaking and I relied on the help of my friends. Recovery was so gradual that it was barely noticeable and I sank into a black abyss of depression. Then, unexpectedly, I connected with a profound inner wisdom, throwing a different light onto what had shaped me as a human being and woman. My hope was rekindled although it was painful to realise that whatever I had done before belonged to the past. It was as if I had become a different person and I had no idea what to do in the future.

There was no way of foreseeing if or when I would be able to return to work. Recalling some of my childhood ambitions, it made sense to me to explore them and see where they would take me. Eventually, I enrolled in a drama class, though it quickly dawned on me that my acting abilities did not match exactly those of the leading ladies of stage and screen. Apart from that, being able to remember one's lines is definitely essential – and that had proved to be a bit of a struggle.

On reflection, it occurred to me that what I really wanted to do was to sing, paint and write. After taking a few private singing lessons, I attended jazz singing classes at a renowned Adult Education institute for five years. It was exhilarating and did wonders for my self-confidence as well as for my social life.

Concurrently, I unleashed my inner painter when I joined a local art group. My mother had been against my studying art because, so she told me, "artists starve and sleep under bridges". Did she have a point? Perhaps she did as my art by no means resembles that of Renoir and the like. Nevertheless, I discovered my penchant for the abstract and am rather proud of my artistic endeavours, which were admired by everyone in the group.

Joy and my sense of humour had started to make a comeback and after joining a creative writing group I became even more alive. It was like getting to know yet another self and a new purpose: I wanted to write a book. In fact, I did publish a self-help e-book a few years ago. Yet with time it dawned on me that I wanted my next book to be if not funny, at least amusing. When I re-remembered some of my life's little comedy moments, and shared them with my friends their suggestion was to publish them. I decided to do just that and could not have done it without the help of my innovative tutor.

One of the most important lessons my experience has taught me is that we need to have some light relief from the trials and tribulations life throws at us occasionally. What better way to do this than by finding something that uplifts us and brightens our day? I hope the stories you are about to read will do exactly that and that they make you smile, or even laugh, just as much as they did when I wrote them.

London 2019

A BIG THANK YOU

to Michael Loveday and Yvonne de Valera

for their help with the creation of this book.

Contents

PLAYING "SUMMER"

It was a cold winter's day in January 1953. The sky was grey and heavy with snow, with flakes waiting to fall and cover everything with a white, shimmering blanket. Outside, people were tightening the collars of their coats and holding on to them with one hand, while keeping the other in their pocket as they were hastening along the street. Inside our apartment it was cosy and warm and the drops of condensation on the window panes were slowly trickling down the glass onto the glossy white wooden frames and then onto the wide polished marbled ledge.

My parents had gone shopping, leaving the door ajar so that my Godmother, who lived opposite and whose door was also left open, could pop in and check on my sister and me (she was five and I was two and a half). Alternatively, we were able to just wander across, usually carrying a selection of toys and books which we would scatter all over her living room floor. There we would crouch and play, or listen to her never ending flow of fairy tales.

I adored my godmother, though sadly never got to know her that well. She was calm and kind with sparkling green eyes and there was an air of elegance around her. She occasionally delighted us with chocolate-flavoured boiled sweets - and where she managed to find them is still a mystery to me. East Germany was under Soviet rule and sweets were a rarity.

On that particular day unbeknownst to her, we obviously got bored with our dolls and teddy bears and, having a vivid imagination as children do, we designed a game of our own. We did that sometimes. We would rummage in our parents' wardrobes, trying on our mother's dresses and shoes or our father's jackets and ties. To complete our attire, we would apply some of my mother's lipstick onto our cheeks and lips before we stuck an unlit cigarette in our mouths to look like "proper" adults. Then we would pose in front of the mirror and act as if we were grown-ups.

However, that's not what we did on that day. The game we played was quite different. It was so different, in fact that it aroused a lot of interest in the street below and when my parents returned home, they were surprised to find a group of spectators gathered outside our house. They were gazing up at the building, and some onlookers were amused and chuckled whereas others were clearly dismayed and disapproved of what they saw.

My parents were curious as to what everyone was staring at, and as they cast their eyes up, they stopped at our bay window in shock and disbelief at what they witnessed: two little girls covered in brown shoe polish and wearing nothing but sun glasses, prancing about happily on the inside ledge, laughing and waving and blowing kisses at the people below. Suffice it to say, that the two little girls were my sister and me.

They quickly left the scene, rushed into the house and up the stairs. My father came in first, followed by my mother and godmother, whose cheeks were somewhat flushed presumably because my mother had had words with her for leaving us unsupervised for too long. Consequently she hadn't had a clue what we had got up to.

Still giggling, as we were having so much fun on our make-belief beach with our pretend suntans and enjoying the public attention, we greeted them happily. They didn't exactly share our sentiment. The expression on my father's face was stern.

"What are you doing up on the window ledge? You could slip on the towel and fall and hurt yourself. Apart from that, why in heaven's name are you naked? What will people think? And why have you smeared shoe polish all over your bodies?"

He firmly ordered us to come down at once. My sister and I didn't quite understand why they were so angry when we were clearly having such a good time. We beamed first at him and then at our mother and godmother. They had just stood there, amazed and lost for words.

"We were playing summer!" we answered in unison, before we climbed down onto the chair we had put in front of the window ledge.

The three of them couldn't help but burst out with laughter. Then my mother ushered us to the bathroom, trying to wash the shoe polish off our bodies. She didn't quite manage it and the pale brown stains were a reminder of our "Playing Summer" game on a miserable winter's day and amused us – and hopefully the bystanders for weeks to come.

YELLOW CUCUMBERS

The year was 1953 and it was the day before Christmas Eve. I was just under four years old when my mother, father and I fled from Russian-occupied East Germany. Apparently, they had already started planning their escape because my father especially had been under mounting pressure from the State Security Police, also known as the "Stasi", to spy on colleagues and neighbours and inform the Stasi of any suspected pro-Western attitudes and activities. As persistent as the Stasi were, so was my father's refusal to oblige and on the 23rd December my parents were tipped off that their arrest was imminent. We left at a few minutes notice with only the clothes we were wearing. I had so been looking forward to seeing my sister who had been staying with my maternal grandmother some fifty miles away, and to helping our mother to decorate the Christmas tree.

There was something else I was also looking forward to and that was to getting our annual orange. The choice of food available was very limited and I've no idea where my father managed to find oranges, but he did and it was one of the highlights of Christmas. There was something about an orange that fascinated me. I liked its colour and would not eat it for days, gently stroking its dimpled skin and breathing in its aroma in amazement.

I would get my orange, albeit not in the usual manner. I knew something serious was going on, though being so young I was unable to fathom the enormity of my parents' situation and the risk they, as well as their friend, were about to take.

There was a likelihood of them being watched and if the three of us left together, it might arouse suspicion. It had to appear as if we were doing some last minute Christmas shopping. Hence, our good-byes were brief as if we really were just popping to the shops – just not together.

So there we were, my father and I in his friend's car, driving to the only tram stop in East Berlin that had remained open and was used by commuters who had jobs in West Berlin. My mother would make her own way a little later. Riding on the tram was quite a dangerous undertaking in itself as there were regular controls by the Stasi to ensure the passengers were all legitimate workers and not defectors. Thankfully, nobody came to check our papers.

Once in West Berlin, we spent the night with a relative of my East German Grandmother before boarding a plane to Frankfurt. The arrangements for our onward journey had been made quickly and shortly after landing, another relative handed my father train tickets to Gelsenkirchen, a mining town in North-Rhine Westphalia, and the fare for the tram from the railway station to his parents' house.

It had been very traumatic to leave so hastily and without my mother and sister, and on some level I had sensed my father's fear. I too was frightened and cried a lot, whereupon he would cuddle me and tell me that we were going to visit my other Grandfather and Grandmother, a prospect which alleviated my fear and really excited me.

We were travelling for many hours. My father was subdued and most likely as hungry and tired as me, but he had no money left to buy us something to eat.

We both watched the rain pelting against the window panes and every time I told him that I was hungry and asked "Are we there yet?" he would answer: "We will be there very soon, my little Clia" ('Clia' was his pet name for me.) The thought of meeting my Grandpa in particular (I didn't have one back home) kept my hunger at bay; at least until the lady and her son sitting opposite us, unwrapped some door-stop sandwiches, filled with sausage and cheese. My eyes must have almost popped out of their sockets at the sight and I got up from my seat to inspect them.

"Oh" I said to the woman "they look yummy" or words to that effect. She glanced first at me and then at my father.

"Are you hungry?"

"Very" I replied "We haven't eaten for a long while and my daddy has no money". Again, she glanced at my father and softly asked him if we were from the "East".

"Yes" he replied quietly and when while listening to the story of our escape, she got out a pocket knife, cut the sandwiches in half and handed them to us. To my absolute delight, she even had an orange, which she also shared with us.

We arrived at my Grandparents' house in the early evening on Christmas eve and I loved them both instantly as much they loved me. That was a good thing because my father departed the next morning and I – and my sister who left East Germany on a visitor's visa in our other Grandmother's passport and never returned – would not be reunited with our parents until the following December. By that time they were settled in Frankfurt and were able to offer us a comfortable home.

Residing also with my grandparents were my father's sister, my Aunt Mia, her bad tempered husband Uncle Alfred whom I made every effort to avoid and his son Peter from a previous marriage. Peter was a few years older than my sister and me and watched over us.

Apart from that, there were Rita, a small-ish dog of a non-descript breed, who usually snarled when I was approaching, and Senta, the Alsatian, who was gentle but too much for my elderly Grandfather to handle, so to my upset he was forced to find her another home.

Aunt Mia had been unable to have children of her own and we bonded quickly. She had many talents, one of which was that she could make beautiful clothes even out of a pair of tatty old curtains, which she cut up, and turned into some pretty dresses for me. Despite my tender years, I was already fashion conscious and the mere idea of wearing dresses made out curtains horrified me, yet it so happened that luckily, they were my favourite outfits.

My grandparents and Aunt Mia made sure I (and later my sister) didn't want for anything. Chocolate was a luxury and my grandmother would get me to play hide-and-seek with a handful of raisins, which she would put somewhere in the kitchen cupboard and I had to find them. At weekends she cooked for all of us and kept me entertained by telling me stories, while peeling a large amount of potatoes, chopping vegetables from my Grandfather's allotment or kneading the dough for a delicious apple crumble.

My grandfather enjoyed gardening and watching things grow. He lovingly tended to the flowers in the back garden of the house and frequently took me along with him to the allotment on the other side of the street. He grew a variety of vegetables and I would help him pick green beans or tomatoes and have fun watering the vegetables, usually giving him a little watering too. When the carrots were in season, he pulled one out of the moist earth, held it under the tap to rinse off the soil and handed it to me to try. I carefully took a small bite. It was very crunchy and kind of sweet though decided there and then, that carrots were weird and that they were to be eaten cautiously and not too often. They didn't exactly become my favourite vegetable, though I eat plenty of them now, steamed rather than raw.

Aunt Mia and Uncle Alfred had their own living quarters in the apartment although I only tended to go there when Uncle Alfred was out. One afternoon Aunt Mia called me and my Grandparents to come in, saying she had a surprise for me. She was carrying a couple of big shopping bags and smiled happily.

We all sat down, wondering what the surprise could be.

"I have a very special treat for you, Cornelia" she said.

"Oh," I trilled and clapped my little hands together. "Did you get me some chocolate?"

"No, my darling. I bought you something much better than chocolate. I am sure you will like it".

I was disappointed. My imagination didn't stretch much further than chocolate, and I could not believe that whatever she had bought for me could taste better than chocolate or possibly chocolate-flavoured ice cream. Not even my grandmother's apple crumble could compete.

She proudly reached deep into the bag and held up something so peculiar that it made me laugh out aloud. Until then I had thought that carrots were one of Nature's strange inventions, but what she had bought me was even stranger. There were a few of them, maybe four or five. Yellow they were – and curved and not like anything I had ever seen before. I stared at them and let my eyes wander around the room. Everybody was smiling and really pleased with her purchase.

"What are they?" I asked my Aunt.

"These are bananas, sweetie. They are fruit that come from far, far away." she said. I was confused.

"Bananas?" I repeated, somewhat confused. "What do you do with them?" I wanted to know.

"You eat them, Cornelia." She broke one off the bunch and gave it to me with a warm smile on her face. I eyed it suspiciously as well as curiously wondering how something like that could taste as good as or perhaps better than chocolate. It just didn't seem possible. I turned it around and shifted it from one hand to the other and then inspected all sides thoroughly before running my fingers over its skin. It was smooth and pleasant to touch. Then I held it to my nose. Its smell was different to that of any other fruit I knew and I wasn't sure if I liked it or not.

It was beyond me why anyone would want to eat such a strange looking thing, but I put it to my mouth and bit into the bit where it had been separated from the bunch. It was tough and scratchy and hurt the roof of my mouth. I was not impressed. Everybody had been watching me and they were amused by my reaction.

"How can anybody eat that? It's not very nice."
"The banana is inside and people do eat it." my aunt said and tapped against it.
"Ohhh. But how do you get to it?"
"You peel it." she explained. I inspected the banana even more closely. "How do I do that?" I asked.

She gently took it from my hand, broke off the top into which I had bitten, and peeled it, leaving half of it covered. It was extraordinary and made me giggle because now I could see the fruit and it wore what almost resembled a skirt. She then handed it back to me and I bit off a small piece, chewing it unenthusiastically and expecting it to melt in my mouth like chocolate. It didn't. I pulled a face and spat it out. "I don't like these yellow cucumbers" I declared and they all laughed out aloud.

I didn't eat another banana for a long while and if anybody had told me that bananas would become the most popular fruit in the world, I would not have believed them. Nor would I have believed that they would become a staple part of my diet in later years. To me they were just *yellow cucumbers*.

MY BABY BROTHER

My hands gripped the squares of the mesh metal fence tightly as I watched Herbert, the nine year old son of the local greengrocer, and his mates play in his parents' garden. It wasn't really a garden as such but rather a large square of dark earth with narrow flower bed borders and a large sycamore tree. Herbert's real pride and joy, however, was the play hut with a boldly grinning wooden Micky Mouse above the door, welcoming those who entered it with open arms. A team effort, Herbert and his friends – with a lot of help from his father, a DIY enthusiast - had cut it out of a sheet of hard board with a coping saw and nailed it to the roof.

They were often making things, Herbert and his pals. Once they'd even made a miniature train station complete with station master and little people on the platform, all painted in bright colours.

On that particular day they were dressed as pirates, complete with eyepatches and bandanas and they were laughing and talking with funny accents. My eyes followed their every move as they carefully applied gold paint to the blades of their wooden swords to get ready for some serious play.

I was seven and it was obvious to me that they were having a lot more fun playing *boys'* games than I was having playing *girls'* games. I longed to join in.

"Herbert?" I meekly called his name but he was too busy putting the finishing touches to his sword and hadn't heard me.

"Herbert?" I called again, a little louder than before.

He turned around.

"Yes Cornelia? What is it?"

"Can I please come and play with you?"

"What? You want to play with *us*? But you are a girl and we play *boys'* games. *Girls* are not allowed in our club."

"Ooh. Please, please, let me play with you," I begged.

"No, sorry, it's strictly for boys," he insisted. "Why don't you play with your dolls like the other girls?" he asked, as he pivoted on his heel and grinned at his mates.

"I don't like playing with dolls. It is really boring. I like the games you play. So please, please let me play with you."

Herbert was unmoved by my pleas. My bottom lip began to quiver and I could feel tears welling up in my eyes.

It wouldn't be the only time I was told girls should do, well, what girls were meant to do in the mid-Fifties and even in later years. Playing football with some of my class mates at secondary school earned me a bad reputation. Then I wanted to swap needlework for handicrafts and woodwork. I loathed needlework. I was no good at it and failed to see the point of it. The headmaster firmly denied my request on the grounds that *'Handicraft and woodwork classes were for boys'* and when a shy and sensitive pupil from my class wanted to attend cookery classes rather than woodwork, the headmaster had a similar reply for him. Cookery classes – as well as needlework - were supposed to prepare us girls for our role as housewives and mothers and the boy was never going to be a housewife. He might have become a brilliant chef, but alas was not given the chance.

"You are being mean," I said quietly. Herbert just shrugged his shoulders and carried on applying golden paint to the handle of his pirate sword.

I lowered my head and almost burned holes in the pavement with my stare before slowly turning around and walking back toward our house. I sat on the wall outside, wondering what it would take for them to let me join in their play. There was only one solution to the problem: I needed to have a brother. Holding that thought, I rang our door bell and as my mother opened the door, I wasted no time to ask her a very important question.

"Mummy, where do children come from? Does Father Christmas bring them?"

My mother looked at me with astonishment. She didn't answer my question until we were in our living room.

"No, Father Christmas doesn't bring children. That would be the stork. The stork brings them" she repeated. "Why do you want to know?"

"Herbert and his friends won't let me play with them. He said I should play with dolls like other girls but I don't really enjoy playing with dolls. If I had a brother, then maybe he would let me join in with their games. So, what is a stork and what do I have to do for the stork to bring me a brother? Do I write to him like I write to Father Christmas?"

"The stork is a large bird and no, you don't have to write to him. What you need to do is leave a sugar cube on the window ledge, with a green thread tied around it so the stork will know that you want a brother, and not another sister. He'll pick up the sugar during the night but you might have to be patient. He has to visit many families and deliver lots of babies all over the world ".

"Oh. Tying the thread around the sugar cube sounds easy enough. How long do I have to wait then, Mummy?"

"Umm." My mother paused for a few seconds. "That's hard to tell. Only the stork knows that," she said, smiling warmly.

"Do we have any sugar cubes?" was my next question. We didn't – they were dearer than granulated sugar and considered a bit of a luxury. However, she sent me to the grocery shop to buy a box and I practically skipped there. Herbert and his friends were nowhere to be seen when I passed the garden. I couldn't wait to tell them the good news, that soon I would have a brother and that we would both be playing with them.

That evening, I clumsily tied a piece of emerald green cotton thread around a sugar cube and carefully placed it outside on the kitchen window sill. The thought of getting a brother and being included in the boys' games was so enormously thrilling that I lay awake for much of the night.

When morning came, I leapt out of bed and immediately headed for the kitchen. I opened the window to check if the sugar cube had gone, and yes, it had. I could barely contain my excitement and rushed out of our apartment, down the stairs, to the main door.

I expected to find a baby boy, wrapped in a white sheet, on the step, gurgling merrily and reaching out for me. He wasn't there. Then it occurred to me that the stork might have left him outside the backdoor that led to the cellar, so I checked there too. To my utter disappointment, he wasn't there either.

Admittedly, my mother had told me that I might have to wait a while. All the same, having a brother was a matter of great importance and urgency, so I had obviously hoped for and expected immediate results.

For several weeks tying the green thread around the sugar cube at bed time became a ritual. I even put extra cubes on all the other window ledges in case the mice or magpies pinched them and once, when it had rained, I concluded that they must have melted. From then on I wrapped them in grease paper. It had made no difference. Despite my efforts, my disappointment was the same every morning: the sugar had disappeared without a trace but there was no baby brother on the doorstep, waiting to be cradled. I was beginning to think that the stork was very inefficient, not to mention cheeky for taking the sugar and not honouring his duty to me. Every time I moaned to my mother about it and questioned when my brother would come, her answer was the same:

"You have to be patient. It takes time."

"How much more time?"

"That's hard to say, darling. It all depends on the stork. But he has picked up plenty of sugar cubes by now, so he surely has got your message."

A few more weeks went past and, although disillusioned, I prayed every night for the stork to fulfil my wishes. Then, one afternoon as I was heading for the nearby playground, I bumped into Marcus, the son of my mother's best friend, with whom I played only rarely as we usually ended up arguing. Marcus had some unexpected news to share.

"Guess what?"

"What?"

"I now have a brother. His name is Martin. My mum went to hospital and brought him back with her. He has hardly any hair and cries a lot. Would you like to see him?"

"What do you mean – your mum went to hospital and brought him back with her?" I was mystified. As far as I could make out hospitals were for sick people.

"Did you put sugar cubes with a green ribbon on the window sill for the stork?"

"Sugar cubes? No. I didn't." Now it was Marcus' turn to be confused. "So, do you want to come and meet him?"

"Yes. I do," I said and nodded. All kinds of thoughts rushed through my head as we strolled around the corner to the block where he lived. I felt cheated and couldn't help but wonder if the stork had made a dreadful mistake. Perhaps, in reality, Martin was *my* brother.

"What is it like to have a brother, then?" I wanted to know.

"Ugh. I don't know yet. He's so small and he can't even talk." Marcus sounded somewhat miserable.

"Oh." I said and stayed silent after that and so did Marcus.

When we arrived at his parents' apartment (fifth floor, no lift – how did his mother – and others - manage?), Martin was being bathed and I was in for a bit of a surprise. It was the first time in my little life that I became aware of the anatomical differences between boys and girls. It was most intriguing.

Martin was very cute indeed, and, yes he was very small. As I stroked his tiny head, it dawned on me that even if I did have a baby brother he would be just that – a baby. It would be ages until he was old enough to play with Marcus or with me or even with Herbert and his mates. My hopes of ever being allowed to play with them were dashed at once.

I stopped placing sugar cubes on our window ledges. Since the stork had let me down so badly, I wasn't sure if it was safe to carry on believing in him.

Where children came from remained a closely guarded secret until I was 10 when a boy from my neighbourhood (I still remember his name: it was Gerhard) told me that his mother had had a home birth. He was uncertain how this whole "baby thing" happened, but was certain that the stork had nothing to do with it.

Nowadays, children learn about procreation from an early age and the myth of the stork delivering children is no longer passed on. Yet, in some rural areas of Germany, it is still customary to place a large wooden stork on a pole, carrying a nappy-wearing baby, outside a house of newlyweds. Sometimes baby clothes are also hung on a washing line that spans the windows. The same tradition is upheld when a baby has arrived and the pole is also positioned there when a year has gone past and the couple have not produced an offspring. It's quite sweet, really.

I never did get invited to play pirate games with Herbert and his friends; nor did I ever get the brother I so longed to have. However, throughout my life I have had close friendships with men, who were just like brothers to me and to them I was like the sister they had always wanted.

PERFECT DICTION

School wasn't at the top of my list of favourite places to be - at least not when I was six and my excitement of the night before finally going to school was short-lived. Eager to learn how to read and write, above all, I wanted to learn to speak English, a language I had fallen in love with thanks to my father. We lived in Frankfurt, West Germany and he liked listening to Jazz, Blues and Swing, which was mainly played on the American Forces Network, a radio station catering for the American soldiers and their families who were stationed at various locations in the country.

Of course, in my six-year-old naivety it had not occurred to me that learning is a process and knowledge is not acquired momentarily. Hence memories of my first few days at school still stick vividly in my mind.

On day one, I could barely contain myself. I would have run to the big red brick building in the next street had it not been for clutching my 'sugar cone'. Traditionally given when children start school, it is a colourful large cardboard cone filled with sweets, chocolate eggs and practical things like a ruler, eraser, pencils and sharpener. My sugar cone, as far as I remember, was sunflower yellow with large pink roses printed on it and I held on to it tight so as not to drop it.

As I approached the large cast iron gate, crowds of children, a few unaccompanied like me, and others tightly gripping the hands of their mothers, were waiting to be let in. When the school bell rang, the headmistress walked across the yard, unlocked the gate and we were ushered into the sports hall, which had been converted into a cinema for this special occasion. There we sat and watched the movie *Heidi* and there weren't many dry eyes in the auditorium. My guess is that some of the tears were cried by children who were frightened by being in a strange place but the film was engrossing and the sobbing sounds soon stopped.

When the lights came on, the headmistress got up, took to her stand and welcomed us warmly, telling us about the importance of education and her hopes for all of us achieving our highest potential. Her speech was followed by the teachers serving tea and cookies to the adults and lemonade to the pupils-to-be. It was a wonderful treat, certainly for me, as at home we were only allowed to drink water or cordial or milk, which I didn't like then and don't like now.

My excitement was deepened when we were led to our respective class rooms where we were invited to choose a desk. Old they were, still fitted with ink wells and bearing witness to those who had sat there before me and had scratched their names into the wood.

I was rather shy, so naturally opted for a seat in one of the back rows, next to a girl whose name I dimly recollect was Monica. She had the biggest brown eyes I had ever seen and long, shiny ebony curls for which I envied her. We exchanged glances and, not wearing school uniforms, only customary in boarding schools, she curiously inspected my attire.

"Why are you wearing an apron?" she whispered. "You don't need to. That's what they used to do in the olden days."

I blushed. "I didn't realise" came my mortified reply.

I untied the long cotton bands and stuffed the apron in the sugar cone. We didn't get to speak any more. The teacher, Mrs. Becke, cleared her throat and asked us to stop chatting. I thought it was getting serious, and expected books to be handed out. But no, that wasn't so. Instead, each pupil's name was called out and our little hands went up in the air on hearing ours. When she had completed the register, she requested that we come to the front of the room and she taught us a simple, short and easy-to-memorise song, though which one it was has escaped me. We then formed a circle, held hands, sang the song and danced and that was it.

'That's all very nice. But when are we going to learn to read and write and speak English?' I secretly wondered though didn't dare ask. After all, it was only the first day.

The ensuing few days weren't that much different. Mrs Becke read us short stories, which we then discussed. She taught us more, easy-to-memorise ditties, which we sang in a circle, as usual. We drew pictures, cut out shapes and images and made collages and were also introduced to Origami (the Japanese art of paper folding). To say that I didn't enjoy these activities wouldn't be true because I did and they also enabled us children to get to know one another better. However, they reminded me more of kindergarten rather than my idea of school and I was disappointed to say the least.

By Day Four we still hadn't been given any books. I was getting bored and restless. As far as I was concerned, school was over. Halfway through a lesson, I quietly packed my satchel, got up and, with my head bowed, tip-toed toward the door. I could feel the eyes of the other pupils in my back and just as I was about to open the door, Mrs. Becke who had watched me with amazement, addressed me: "Cornelia? Where are you going?" I turned around, raised my head and looked at her.

"I am going home." I said with sadness in my voice. "I thought I was going to learn something here but I haven't. I am bored and I'm going home."

Mrs. Becke, who would become one of my favourite teachers, was speechless and didn't stop me. She knew I would be back. Indeed, when I returned the next day it wasn't exactly of my own volition. My mother insisted and told me in no uncertain terms that all children had to attend school and if they refused the police would come and take them there.

Well, it wasn't the police who took me to school. It was my mother, and it was a one off occasion. She even walked me to the classroom where Mrs. Becke greeted me with a big smile.

Lo and behold, there was a pile of books on her desk that day; real books that smelt new and had not only pictures, but lots of words in them. At home, I bound mine in royal blue paper so it wouldn't get damaged and could be passed on to somebody else when I finished with it.

Learning to read and write came easily to me, and eighteen months later I was a frequent visitor at the library, borrowing on average two books a week, which I read under the stairs in the basement of our house. My books were like friends and it didn't bother me that they were written in German. But in Year 2, when I asked when we would be taught English, I didn't like the answer. "Not till year five, Cornelia. You will have to wait till then".

In the meantime I made futile attempts to speak English the way the American presenters did on the radio, though I was totally clueless as to what they were actually talking about. It was rather frustrating and as neither of my parents spoke much English I eventually abandoned my unsuccessful venture and counted the weeks, months and years until English finally appeared as one of the subjects on the school curriculum.

Time did what time does best: it passed and at last the big day arrived: the teacher gave out English books. It was without a shadow of a doubt one of the most endearing days at school I recall. The book was called *Peter Pim and Billy Ball*. I gently stroked its cover and pressed it to my heart like a long lost treasure. On opening it, I was in awe of all those foreign words that I would soon be able to understand and under my breath I muttered "Finally I am learning something that will be useful to me in the future."

I hadn't felt the same about other subjects like maths or geometry and, later on, physics or chemistry - for the simple reason that I didn't understand any of them. It wasn't for lack of trying. My brain seemed to be more interested and better equipped to paint, read, or write in either German or English (and later French), subjects in which I tended to excel, although by now I've forgotten my French because I have never really used it.

The English lessons gave me a huge thrill and I looked forward to each one. It was my earnest desire to speak the language fluently and perfectly. I avidly listened to the various programmes on AFN, trying to understand what was being talked about and diligently practicing my pronunciation, often in front of a mirror to see if moving my lips differently would affect my articulation. To speak without an accent was an unexplained obsession and when a classmate and I were doing our English homework together, I confided in her about my secret wish to sound just like the Americans. She gave me a questioning look.

"Oh, that is easy. Why don't you just put a hot potato in your mouth?"

Her suggestion puzzled me.

"A hot potato? Whatever for?"

She looked at me rather intensely.

"Well, they kind of mumble a bit, don't they? That's what it sounds like to me, anyway. When you speak English with a hot potato in your mouth, I am sure you will sound totally American then. You better leave the skin on though," she insisted. "Otherwise the potato will break into pieces. "

For the sake of achieving perfect diction, I took her advice and dutifully boiled a small potato in its skin. I briefly held it under the cold tap, ceremoniously put it in my mouth and then tried to utter a sentence in English. It took no longer than two seconds for me to have to admit that a) it was very difficult to speak in any language with a hot – or even cold - potato in one's mouth and b) that it had burned my tongue and the roof of my mouth forcing me to spit it out as quickly as possible.

My pronunciation got better just the same, especially with the help of my head teacher at Secondary Modern School, Mr.

Bock whose elocution was excellent. I also liked British pop music and memorised the lyrics of all my favourite songs. My flair for languages had become apparent and Mr. Bock advised my parents that it would be a shame not to make good use of my inherent gift. After finishing school they consequently sent me to one of the world's leading language school in the seaside town of Bournemouth to study Cambridge English and obtain a certificate of proficiency. That, they told me would assist me in securing a good job on my return. It did more than that. In fact, my stay there would determine my future, as some years later I moved to London, improving my English language skills even more, including my pronunciation.

Having lived here for over four decades, only hard core linguists and my best friend can occasionally detect a slight accent and have a notion that I was not born and raised here. There also have been some awkward situations during my time in England and while travelling, when it has actually been advantageous to pass as a native.

28

HOW TO CURE
A COMMON COLD

"I know how you can get rid of your cold really quickly," my friend Eva said, looking all superior, wise and knowledgeable. She lived across the road and I had sauntered there for a bit of sympathy as I felt rather sorry for myself. I sat on her bed and we were chatted, about the latest fashion trends while I sneezed five or six times in quick succession. The tip of my nose was the colour of a ripe tomato and it was very sore from blowing it so many times. My sister had joked that I should join the trumpet orchestra at my school. I wasn't amused. My head was thumping and Eva's voice like everyone else's sounded muffled and it was as if I was immersed in water. Eva handed me a few tissues as I was about to sneeze yet once again and repeated what she had said before.

"Trust me. I really know how you can get rid of your cod quickly". She sounded as if she was about to impart a closely guarded secret to me. I stretched out on her bed.

"Don't keep me in suspense, Eva. I feel so awful and getting through school today was a huge struggle. I could do with spending the day at home tomorrow but I don't think my mother will let me."

"Ah. What's happening tomorrow? It wouldn't be a Maths test by any chance?"

I was amazed. "How did you guess?"

"Well, sometimes people get sick before or even after an ordeal. I read it in one of my Mum's magazines. You hate Maths. Maybe you are so nervous of getting bad grades that your body wanted to have a cold so you didn't have to go to school. "

"Eva! Honestly. The things you come out with. You astound me. Yes, I hate Maths - because I just don't get it hence am no good at it. My brain seems to go on strike during the lessons with Mr. Wolf. I find his way of teaching dull and I just don't understand what he is trying to teach us. "

"Yes, you're right. He is not the most exciting of tutors. I fell asleep once during a history lesson he gave when our history teacher was on holiday. Nevertheless, doing your homework and opening your books on occasion would help."

"Yeah, yeah. Thanks for the lecture. I do try, honestly. Now just tell me how I can get rid of this blasted ~~this~~ cold. I certainly can't see myself even get a D in the test feeling the way I do. So what do I need to do?" No sooner had I asked there was a ticking sensation in my nostrils and I sneezed another loud "Achoo" into my tissue.

"Gesundheit," Eva uttered. "It's something the ancient Greeks used, I believe."

"So? What is it then? What do I need to do?"

"All you need to do is eat raw Garlic".

"Raw garlic?"

"Yes, raw garlic. Seven cloves. I read it in one of the women's magazines and I am certain you will feel a lot better tomorrow if you do that."

"Seven? Yuk. That sounds a bit excessive. Are you sure?"

Eva reflected on my question for a brief moment. "Um. I think that is what was recommended in the article."

"Does it have to be seven? Why can't it be five?"

"I can't remember the exact reason now. I do recall the article talked about the ancient Greeks using a lot of natural remedies and one of them was garlic, which they used to cure the common cold. Oh. Wait. Apparently, it's also very good for your blood."

"If you say so. I'm not totally convinced though. Have you still got the magazine? I want to see it for myself."

Eva disappeared in her parents' living room and there was a sound of her flicking through a stack of magazines. "I can't find it" she called "but it definitely mentioned seven cloves of garlic".

Armed with her advice and a few spare tissues, I went back home and immediately made my way to the kitchen where my mother was trimming the fat off a loin of pork, getting it ready to place it in the large saucepan where onions were already frying in butter. I could hardly smell anything though the same didn't apply to our miniature schnauzer Trixie, who sat, looking all expectantly, hoping for titbits.

"Hello Cornelia" my mother greeted me. "How are you feeling?"

"Really rough, mum." I sniffled. "I don't think I can go to school tomorrow."

"Why don't we wait till morning and see how you feel then?"

"OK." I replied and headed for the larder, where I looked in the vegetables baskets. "Tell me, do we have any garlic?"

"Garlic? Whatever for? You don't like it, but yes there should be a bulb in the brown paper bag."

"Eva told me I should eat seven cloves of raw garlic and my cold would be gone."

My mother stifled a smile. "I see. And how does she know this?"

"She read it in one of her mother's magazines. It's an ancient Greek thing, she told me."

"Yes, they were very smart, the ancient Greeks. They used a lot of herbs and whatever Nature provided. In fact, there was a remarkable doctor by the name of Hippocrates and one of his famous quotes was: 'Let food be thy medicine and medicine be thy food.' Therefore, I don't doubt that raw garlic is a good remedy to treat a cold although I don't quite believe that it has to be seven cloves. Heaven only knows what they will do to your insides, dear." She stifled another smile. "Still, it's just a cold. It will pass."

"Yes, and I want it to pass rapidly because it's making me very miserable." I commented while counting the number of cloves of the bulb in my hand. The words "Perfect, exactly seven" passed my lips. I peeled off the skin with a small kitchen knife, and put the cloves on a saucer. "How do you think I should eat them? Bite into them?" I wondered.

"Why don't you grate them and if you want my advice, don't eat the whole lot."

I duly grated the garlic and then petted Trixie before going upstairs, up to the room I shared with my sister. I switched on the radio and, holding the aerial with one hand, managed to get a vaguely decent reception of Radio Caroline, the British pirate radio station broadcasting from the North Sea. The station played all my favourite English and American pop songs whereas German radio stations played hardly any and I didn't always like what was on the American Forces Network's playlist. I cautiously eyed the small mound of mashed garlic, braced myself and put some on a teaspoon and slowly put it in my mouth. The moment it touched my tongue, it was a shock to my taste buds and I wanted to spit it out. It was pungent and spicy and I did not enjoy its flavour one iota. Still, if it worked, then that would be fine, even if I had to suck a large number of mints to disguise my breath. I ate it all and expected my symptoms to be alleviated or even disappear in an instant. They didn't. Well, not exactly anyway. It took a while until the effect of the garlic kicked in and shortly after dinner, my stomach was making a lot of gurgling noises, which disrupted my (and my sister's) precious sleep. With hindsight, I wished I had followed my mother's advice.

Early the next morning my father came in, with Trixie in tow. She usually leapt on to the bed to greet me. However, that morning she wouldn't come near me. She stuck her nose in the air, let out a short yelp and quickly ran out of the door.

As my father came closer, he looked at me. "What is that smell?" he asked. "It smells like a garlic farm in here."

"Is it that bad?" I wanted to know, while holding one hand in front of my mouth and checking my breath. It *was* that bad. "It's not just your breath. Your whole body exudes an odour that is quite unpleasant." he remarked.

"Oh no, that's terrible. It's the seven cloves of raw garlic I ate to get rid of my cold and I think it's had some effect." I did, as a matter of fact feel better.

" Whoever told you to do that forgot to mention that you would reek of the stuff. You can't possibly go to school smelling like you do." my father insisted.

"But, dad, we have a math test today."

"You will have to miss it. Otherwise you will sit in a classroom by yourself. Don't worry, there will be another one, Clia" (Clia was his pet name for me).

"Oh. If you say so."

My relief at his suggestion was immense and for the next two days I enjoyed lazing around in the garden and waiting for my body odour to return to normal. I even consulted my math book ÷reluctantly, I might add - despite thinking that I was going to miss the test.

Back at school I learned that the maths test had been postponed until the following week as Mr. Wolf was unwell. Apparently, he had a severe cold. I felt sorry for him, more so when I mused whether he too ate raw garlic to combat it. Whatever the case might have been, from my recollections, I didn't get another cold for a very long time, so the ancient Greeks definitely were onto something.

DREAM LOVER

The dark stained wooden stairs creaked loudly as I followed my best friend Helga up to her sister's old bedroom where I would be spending the night. Thankfully, it was summer—the house was around two hundred years old and lacked central heating. Even the fan heaters in the corner of every room couldn't take away the chill of winter and the warmest place was the kitchen on the ground floor.

My friendship with Helga had started two years previously, when I was 14 and she 16. Her widowed mother owned an old-fashioned grocery store and delicatessen in the small spa town bordering on our agricultural village on the outskirts of Frankfurt. I usually passed there on my way to the outdoor pool and one day, as I was walking past, a black and white Spitz shot out of the side entrance and ran toward me. Thinking that he had come to greet me, I leaned down to stroke the dog, whereupon he growled and nipped me in the calf. I lost my footing and fell onto the cobblestone lane. Having witnessed the incident from inside, Helga rushed out to make sure I was okay.

"I am so sorry" she said as she helped me back on my feet. "He isn't the friendliest dog in the world but once he gets to know you, he is like a pussycat" she assured me with a big smile. I wasn't entirely sure if that was true.

"Oh, don't worry. I'll survive," I replied and gently rubbed my leg. "We have a dog too: a miniature Schnauzer, called Trixie and maybe next time your dog sees me, he will realise that I am definitely a dog person."

Again, she smiled and gave me a quizzical look with her sea-green eyes.

"Why don't you come in for a coffee and a piece of our home made cheese cake or whatever else you fancy?" she asked.

I happily accepted her invitation and entered the dimly lit shop. As I stood in front of the display cabinet and cast my eyes over mouth-watering cheeses and a large selection of sausages, making up my mind was difficult. It was a toss-up between a French cheese with little holes in it on a crispy fresh bread roll – oddly, cheese with holes was the only type I ate – or *real* Frankfurter Sausages. Made to a traditional recipe by only one company in the whole of Germany, they were – and I believe still are– wrapped in soft, thin white paper with blue slightly slanted print. They smelt and tasted slightly smoked and were absolutely delicious. My choice was an obvious one as my mother insisted on buying *Vienna* sausages from the recently opened supermarket. They were cheaper but I didn't care for them much as there was something amiss in their flavour.

From then on Helga invited me in whenever she spotted me stroll past and before too long I had become a regular visitor at her house. We would sit in the kitchen, where we talked and laughed – she had the gift of making people laugh – and where she regularly fed me Frankfurters and cheese with holes in it.

Our age difference did not bother her and we soon became close friends. That evening of walking up her stairs we had celebrated Helga's 18th birthday. It was the first party I had ever been to and most of her friends had put in an appearance. There must have been around twenty of us crammed into the living room, singing and dancing or just chatting. The party finished around midnight and since my father had been unable to collect me, it had been agreed that I would be staying over. He didn't like the idea of me walking home alone at night – 25 minutes up a fairly steep hill that was flanked by fields and fruit orchards on the left and just a scattering of houses dotted randomly on the right.

Actually, I liked sleepovers. It was more fun than sharing a bedroom with my sister with whom I didn't get along that well. Our different musical tastes – she liked opera and I pop music –

didn't help matters as we usually argued about who would get to use the one record player we owned between us.

We reached the second floor and the hinges of Helga's sister's old bedroom door screeched as she opened it.

"The hinges need oiling," she mumbled and I could not have agreed more. She turned on the light and we stepped inside.

"Welcome to your boudoir," she said and smiled. I looked around the small and sparsely furnished, yet cosy, room. Two old family photos in black frames graced the newly painted walls. Below them was a white sink with a cold water tap and above the sink there was a small electric immersion heater. There was a single bed, a bedside table with a lamp on it, a wardrobe and a chair by the window plus a blow heater, should the temperatures drop.

Helga took the duvet, pillows and sheets out of the wardrobe, while I put my washbag and pyjamas on the chair and placed my transistor radio on the bedside table. Together we made up the bed and talked about how much fun the evening had been and how much everybody had enjoyed it. Her friends were an interesting bunch including a talented artist whose work impressed my parents so much that they bought some of it, a film production student, a fashion photographer and a chap who wanted to be a pilot like his father. Conversing with some of them had broadened my view on possible future careers, even though my main aspiration at the time was to work in television.

I gazed out of the window and cast my eyes to the star-spangled sky above. Seeing the stars always had a magical effect on me. There wasn't much light pollution then and the myriad stars of the Milky Way − Earth is situated in one of its spiral arms − were bright and still clearly visible.

"Do you think there is life on other planets?" I mused out aloud.

"It can't be ruled out" she said and yawned. "But I am too tired to contemplate aliens. I have just about enough energy to get some oil for the hinges." She made a quick exit, returning quite promptly with a small metal bottle. There was a squirting sound and a faint smell of oil.

"Voila" she said with a satisfied tone as she swung the door back and forth at a rapid speed. "Listen to that! Not a whisper!"

"That's grand" I replied. "Let's just hope I can avoid the creaking stairs if I have to go to the bathroom in the middle of the night." It was next to her mother's bedroom on the floor below.

"Oh, never mind. She's used to the sound, and doesn't hear it anymore. Anyway, it's late and I need to put my head down. I've got be up early in the morning to help Mum with a delivery. Lucky you, you don't have to get up on Saturdays and can sleep late. Good night, Connie. Sleep well."

"You too, Helga. It was such a great party, so thanks for a wonderful evening." She stifled another yawn, half shut the door and then opened it again.

"Oh, and by the way, try and remember your dreams."

I was puzzled. "Why?" I wanted to know.

"Well, whatever you dream when you sleep in a strange bed for the first time comes true," she answered and winked at me.

"Really?" I asked though wasn't entirely convinced. I hadn't any of that kind by then. Yes, there had been a few occasions where my dreams had been bizarre and puzzled me. Whenever that was the case, I would tell my Grandmother about them to see if she could help me understand them. She usually consulted some well-thumbed gypsy dream book, which she held dear and which was published in the 1930s.

It was a fascinating source of some useful and, well, some totally useless information. More often than not the explanations made no sense and didn't sound remotely believable to me.

It wasn't until my late Twenties that I began to grasp the importance and significance of dreams. Inspired by the pioneering work of the eminent Swiss psychiatrist Carl Jung, I delved deeper into their analysis and interpretation. By then, I had had a few dreams of future events that came true but alas they weren't always of the pleasing kind.

"Oh yes, absolutely. See you in the morning," she answered.

"Yes, but hang on a minute. Are you just making this up"?

"Of course not, it's an old proverb".

"I've never heard that one before. That doesn't mean it's true though, does it?"

"Maybe not, but I once had a dream that came true, when we were on holiday in Spain."

"What was it about?"

"I'll tell you another time."

"Hahaha. Don't make me laugh. You are just saying that, aren't you? Besides, what if I have a nightmare?"

"That won't happen. Trust me. Dreams are always nice on the first night," she assured me and left.

I wasn't certain of it and lay awake for quite a while, listening to music and staring pensively at the beams on the ceiling. What would my dreams be about? Would they be about far away exotic destinations I would travel to some day? Would I dream about my future husband or finding fulfilment and fame in a job I loved? Was I going to be shown a beautiful house I would live in and which was furnished as it was in my imagination? Was it possible that I could see the six lotto numbers that would win my family the jackpot or maybe I could even dream of the questions of the forthcoming exams, enabling me to revise only what was necessary?

There was a mishmash of pictures in my head and the prospect of having one or even more pleasurable dreams and letting me have a glimpse of the future was exciting. Hopefully

I would be able to remember what I had dreamed. I closed my eyes and fell into a deep sleep almost instantly.

A stray sunbeam tickling my nose and the smell of freshly made coffee woke me up the next morning. Still very sleepy, I rubbed my eyes and bolted upright in bed. I did so because I actually recalled my dream, though not in detail and an astonishing one it had been. It wasn't a nightmare, no, but it had been extraordinary to say the least and I couldn't wait to tell Helga about it. I splashed cold water on my face and brushed my teeth, threw on my clothes and rushed downstairs into the kitchen.

"Good morning, beautiful. So, how did you sleep? Any dreams you would like to share?" Helga piped merrily.

"Morning. Gosh, I slept like a baby, Helga and yes, I did have the weirdest of dreams."

" Weird? In what way. No wait, let me guess. You dreamed you were going into politics and running the country!" she chuckled. We shared many interests, but politics wasn't one of them.

"Yeah, right. I can see it now." I quipped and grimaced.

"Come on, don't keep me in suspense. What was it about?"

" Well, I am still in shock. Would you believe it? I dreamt I was married to Mick Jagger and we had twins. I mean, Mick Jagger of all people!"

"No way! How did you meet? Where were you living? Were they identical twins?"

"Haven't got a clue. All I recall is that he and I were married and that we had twins. The rest is shrouded in mist."

"Must be wishful thinking, or something like that".

"No. Definitely not" I said thoughtfully. "I am into the Rolling Stones in a big way and I don't find Mick Jagger remotely attractive".

"Many girls would disagree with you. He's definitely got charisma."

41

"He does, I agree. Nevertheless, he doesn't appeal to me."

"Don't rule it out completely," Helga advised me. "You're only 16 and should you meet when you're in your twenties, you might feel differently."

"You could be right. I guess, only time will tell, but, no, honestly, I can't see it. As for having twins, I can't see that either. It sounds like a lot of hard work to me."

"Well, if you do marry him, promise you'll invite me to the wedding." Helga said cheerfully. "Now, on another note, what would you like for breakfast - Frankfurters or scrambled eggs?"

"Scrambled eggs would be lovely, thanks," was my reply, as I poured myself a cup of coffee and made myself more comfortable on the wooden bench.

The years passed, as they do and Helga infrequently teased me about the dream, asking if my path had crossed with Mick's and if she could be maid of honour. They never did – not even during more than two decades I spent working in the music industry in Germany as well as in London when I met many successful British and American groups, with The Rolling Stones being one of the exceptions.

In fact the closest I ever came to meeting Mick Jagger was at a wake for a dear friend of mine in 1990 when I stood next to his then girlfriend, the model Jerry Hall, with whom he went on to raise four children, albeit none of them twins. We were at the buffet where we exchanged smiles while she passed me a plate, knife and fork and a serviette. She then pointed at the potato salad and recommended I try it.

As for me, I didn't marry a rock star nor was I blessed with motherhood. The only children that have passed through my life were other people's and extraordinarily, one couple do have identical twin boys with whom I have spent a lot of time when they were small.

Having said that, dreams have never ceased to fascinate me and keeping a record of them has become a habit. As I write them down, their connotations often become obvious. I also own several dream dictionaries that act as aides with their interpretation and significance. Nonetheless, since being married to a rock star or having twins were none of my aspirations the deeper meaning of that particular dream has remained a mystery to this day.

THE LEGACY

Wolfgang, my brother-in-law stopped the car outside the house my family had lived in for five years while my sister Bess and I were teenagers. We were actually on our way to another village not that far away where Bess was going to recite some of her poetry. Knowing how much I had loved and missed our old house, Wolfgang had kindly made a detour.

Still sitting in the car, I noticed that the white wooden slatted gate was wide open. For me, it was like an invitation. I got out and listened to the crunching sound of my footsteps, as I slowly walked down the gravelled path toward the house. A few workmen were busy packing away their tools and getting ready to leave. From what I had already seen, the house, once whitewashed was painted candy floss pink and the scaffolding was still erected.

"Excuse me" I said to one of the workmen. "Would you know if anybody is at home?"

"Well, yes, they are at home. Just ring the bell", he answered.

"Thank you", I replied, and then added, "I live in England now but a long time ago my family used to live here and I just happen to be passing through."

"Oh. I see" he said. "So do you live in London?" he asked with curiosity.

"Yes, I do."

"What's it like? I've read a bit about it and it looks like an interesting city. Have you ever seen the queen?" he wanted to know.

"Yes, London is a great city. It has a rich history and beautiful architecture.

There is so much to see and do and yes, as a matter of fact, I have seen the queen once. She was in a chauffeur driven limousine, with her husband, Prince Philip by her side. I waved at her and she waved back. It made my day."

"That's nice. Maybe I'll take my wife there when the kids are a bit bigger." He
paused. "Enjoy your stay here."
"I will. Thank you and I do hope you make it to London one day."
"Yes, one day."
He carried on putting things in his dusty bag and we parted.

It was strangely exciting to approach our old house and I couldn't help but have a good look around. The garden seemed much smaller than I remembered. Transformed by my mother and a professional gardener from a total wilderness into a horticultural masterpiece, it had undergone dramatic changes since our departure. Where once there had been an abundance of flowers and fruit trees, there was now a big lawn. Apart from a few pink rose bushes in full bloom alongside the path, I didn't spot any flowers growing anywhere.

The babbling brook that used to flow through the front garden, and turned into a raging mass of water every time it rained heavily, was now confined to a drain. During warm weather, my sister and I would often sit on the edge, letting the cool water run over our feet. We would daydream, and wonder whether the tiny shimmering metallic stones in the sand were made of gold.

Getting closer to the front steps, I noticed that the towering white birch trees that used to flank either side of the house had been felled. The old apple tree was no longer there either. Its branches almost reached the window panes of our room and it was a place favoured by a nightingale. I recalled the first time I had heard it sing in the early hours of one morning. Its song was so beautiful that it touched something deep inside me.

As I was nearing the front steps leading up to the terrace, I stood still and embarked on a brief journey through the past. I saw my family and friends sit around a wooden table on the terrace, eating delicious food my grandmother had prepared and I heard us chat and laugh. I recounted my sister practicing her scales and arias in our room and me grabbing the radio and disappearing to the bathroom where I could listen to the English pirate station Radio Caroline undisturbed. I saw a picture of us giving our father a miniature schnauzer in a bread basket for Christmas. He hadn't wanted us to get a dog, so we figured if we gave it to him as a present, he couldn't possibly refuse it. He didn't.

I saw myself strolling along the rolling hills and fruit orchards, observing rabbits and deer, which came into our back garden to feed in snowy winters when the ground was frozen. Suddenly there was the image of the gardener building an enclosure for our resident tame hedgehog and her six young, whom my mother had rescued from underneath the shed during torrential downpours. There also were memories of my sister and me spending evenings with the farmers who owned the adjoining fields and who had a smallholding up in the village. There we would each milk "our own" cow and help to bring calves into this world Then we would listen to the farmer and his son playing the zither, while his wife knitted jumpers for them both, and cardigans for us.

The mental images tumbled over one another and made me smile, especially the one about my crush on a blue-eyed, blonde, lederhosen- wearing boy at secondary school. We had never actually spoken and all we ever exchanged were shy glances that made us blush and class mates snigger.

I took a deep breath, climbed up the stairs and rang the bell. The door opened by a few inches and a young boy, aged around nine eyed me suspiciously from top to bottom.

"Good evening." I said and introduced myself. "My name is Cornelia. Many, many years ago my family used to live in this house and I wonder if I could speak to your mother. There is something I would like to ask her."

Again, he stared at me, though more with curiosity rather than suspicion.

"Yes, she is. Just a minute." He left the door slightly ajar. "Mummy?" I could hear him call out inside. "There is a woman here. She says she used to live here and wants to ask you something."

His mother, a very attractive blonde woman with blue eyes and a kind face, appeared a short while later. My introduction was greeted with warmth and she shook my hand.

"Oh. Were you the family that used to get flooded a lot?" she enquired.

"Yes, that was us." I sighed. "It was my job to collect the drowned mice and

rats."

"Yuck. That sounds ghastly."

"Well, it wasn't exactly at the top of my list of fun activities, but it had to be

done," I surmised. We both laughed.

Our conversation started to flow. She had just told me of the extension they had built, and invited me in for a guided tour, when much to my annoyance, my brother in law impatiently hooted. I so had wanted to accept her offer but didn't dare.

"Thank you. I would love to but we are en route and I am a little rushed. I do, however, have a question for you. Is there a horse chestnut tree growing in the back?"

She was astounded. "Do you know something about the chestnut tree? We love it and have often wondered how it got here as there are no horse chestnut trees growing in this area. However, nobody has been able to give us any information about it."

"I know a lot about it." I said and then explained its existence. "I really loved living here and was devastated that we had to move. The removal truck had already left and I bid my farewells, walking around the empty rooms for one last time, and checking all the cupboards to make sure I hadn't left anything behind. Something caught my eye in the furthest corner of one of the cupboards. It was a little chestnut I had picked up somewhere, though am not sure exactly where. I then decided that it was going to be my legacy to this place and planted it in the back garden. My sister watched me in disbelief as I dug a hole in the ground, placed the chestnut in it and added a little water.

'May there be a big chestnut tree growing here one day,' I affirmed earnestly, absolutely convinced that this would be so. My sister just rolled her eyes and shuffled her feet. She thought otherwise.

'It will never take' she told me. 'It is November and we have no idea when the house will be occupied again.' She was getting antsy and ordered me to hurry up because our parents were waiting. I was 18 at the time, so that would have been 38 years ago. You can't imagine how pleased I am to hear that my sister was wrong and that a mighty tree grew from that little, old chestnut."

"That's quite a touching story, Cornelia, if I may call you that. Would you like to see it?" No sooner had she uttered these words, there was another sound of repeated hooting.

"Oh, I would like that very much but unfortunately I must be going. You know," I hastily added, "it was my dream to buy the house some day, but that's not likely now."

Again, my brother in law hooted. It was a long and persistent hoot. We smiled at each other, shook hands and said good-bye.

"If ever you are passing, please feel free to drop in. You are always welcome." she said warmly.

There was a lump in my throat as I thanked her and quickened my pace back down the stairs and down the path to the car. I couldn't wait to break the news to my sister and as we drove off I turned around and managed to catch a narrow glimpse of the chestnut tree. It was in full bloom and seeing my legacy it in its magnificence instilled in me a sense of peace and pride. I've not been back since, but wonder if it is still there.

TRUFFLES

Black or white truffles, as I understand, are the fruit of certain fungi which grow below ground, near the roots of trees. They are a highly prized and sought-after delicacy, and white truffles seem to be the most expensive food anyone can wish to eat. A few thin shavings sprinkled in soup or over a gourmet main course easily costs the diner several thousand pounds. According to *Money Inc.* one Italian white truffle weighing 2.2 pounds sold at auction for the sum of $ 200,000 and was delivered to Macau by an Italian chef.

This story isn't exactly about fungi or mushrooms. It is the extraordinary tale about the relationship between one man and a black pot-bellied pig. This particular type of pig originates from Vietnam and is on the endangered species list. Yet, *Truffles*, so named by his owner because hogs are famed for sniffing out the fungi though equally famed for devouring them, did not come from Vietnam. From what I recall, he came from a farm in Gloucestershire.

The first time I heard about *Truffles* was on a clear, frosty November evening when a few neighbours and friends were having a barbecue outside our Georgian terraced house in London's Bayswater area. It was an event that we held every year on the anniversary of Guy Fawkes and his accomplice's plan to blow up the Houses of Parliament in1605 in order to try and restore a Catholic monarchy. Thus, on the 5th of November each year, or Guy Fawkes Night, bonfires are lit throughout the city and colourful fireworks light up the sky.

We were not able to have a bonfire where we lived but our annual barbecue had become a popular event. The towering sycamore trees and walled flowerbeds separate the private terraces from the main road and block out the noise from four lane traffic. In the background the sound of rockets being fired into the night sky could be heard. Tea lights in jam-jars were lined up on the wall, with the flickering flames giving the site a warm and welcoming ambience and the air was filled with our laughter and the smell of barbecued chicken legs, hamburgers and sausages.

There were usually twelve of us, not counting the children who were running around holding sparklers or playing football or hide and seek and the odd passer-by would stop for a chat and a glass of mulled wine from one of the thermos flasks. Though that night, oddly, the brown-eyed Hugo and his beautiful blonde Danish girlfriend Suzanna did not show up until half past ten. By then the tea lights barely flickered, there were just a few embers left in the barbecue and most of the food had been eaten. Strangely, Hannah walked a few steps behind Hugo and the atmosphere between them was notably strained. Neither looked happy or relaxed and Hugo had the kind of expression on his face that can be seen in children when they have been very naughty and got found out.

They slowly approached our small group and Hugo stopped where I was standing, with Suzanna keeping a distance.

"Is there any food left?" he asked. He cast his eyes over a couple of charred sausages, and equally charred chicken drumsticks, limp salad and half-full tubs of various dips.

"Not much, as you can see. Why are you so late? What happened?" Neither he nor Suzanna replied and remained silent as they divided the food between them and started to eat.

Then Hugo spoke and as he did, Suzanna pulled a face, turned her back on us and moved away. "Yeah. Sorry about that. We had to go somewhere and it took longer than expected."

"Oh yes? Where did you go? Anywhere nice? Something to do with work" I asked.

"Um, we went to Gloucestershire and no, it had nothing to do with work. We went to look at a farm." He lowered his head and stared a hole in the paper plate.

I was confused. "You were looking at a farm in Gloucestershire? Are you thinking of moving there?" I couldn't quite picture it. Hugo was a trendy young man who worked as a talent scout for a major record company and to my knowledge he didn't have the slightest interest in agriculture, nor did Suzanna who was a fashion buyer for an upmarket department store.

After a long pause, he answered my question. "No, we're not moving there. We went there to have a look at a litter of black Vietnamese pot-bellied pigs and I bought one."

I was stunned, thinking he was joking. "You did what?" I asked.

"I bought a black Vietnamese pot-bellied pig" he mumbled, whereupon Suzanna glared at him somewhat angrily and went to join the others.

"Are you completely out of your mind? You live on the first floor in a studio apartment with a sleeping gallery. What on earth do you want with a pig, for crying out loud? Do you have any idea how big they become and that they weigh about seven tons when they are fully grown?" (They don't; I was exaggerating.) "Plus – in case you hadn't realised, a pig is classified as 'live-stock' and you cannot keep 'live-stock' in a flat in Central London. It's illegal."

"No, no, it'll be alright," he tried to assure me. "We've got the roof terrace, so he has plenty of outdoor space and I will house train him and take him for walks every day."

I shook my head. "That is the most ridiculous thing I have ever heard. You are totally mad. How does Suzanna feel about the new addition to your household, anyway? I can't imagine her to be thrilled about sharing her life with a pig. And what about Merlin?" I challenged him.

"Well, Suzanna isn't too happy about it, but it's my flat so I can have whatever pet I want. She'll adapt, I am sure. We've been to see him and he is really cute and from what I have read, pigs are very sociable and friendly and can get on well with cats."

Having said that he strolled toward the others and as he approached, Suzanna loudly and with a sarcastic undertone made the announcement that Hugo had bought himself a pig. Everybody stared at him in disbelief.

"We've shot a video of *Truffles*. Why don't you all come upstairs to watch it?" Hugo added. It was an invitation that we readily accepted. It was getting very chilly and we were curious. As we settled down in their apartment, we got to 'meet' *Truffles*, who, only two weeks old, indeed was a very cute piglet. One couldn't help but like him. Some weeks later he moved in, joining Merlin, Urban the Axolotl – a type of lizard - and Harry the white rat.

Hugo, it has to be said, took excellent care of *Truffles*. He fed him well and even tried to teach him tricks, although I don't recall it being a successful exercise, except that he did get him to stand on his hind legs begging for crisps, which he loved. Every day Hugo carried *Truffles* down the stairs, and up again, because he couldn't manage them and proudly took him for long walks in Kensington Gardens where they created quite a stir. Many people stopped and enquired what breed of dog he was and turned away chuckling when he proudly told them. "It's not a dog. It's a black Vietnamese pot-bellied pig." In fact, *She,* a leading glossy woman's magazine - sadly no longer in existence - even published a photo of the two of them on their back cover.

A few months had gone by. *Truffles* had grown from a cute piglet into a not-quite-as-cute and slowly maturing male hog with, shall we say, certain 'urges'. He adored Hugo and Suzanna though did develop a bit of a jealous streak when the two had visitors and didn't pay him enough attention. He also took great delight to rub himself on their guests' legs and even after he was castrated, he would pee on their feet and had a tendency to bite on more than one occasion. We were all advised to sit cross legged on the bar stools and keep our legs there.

That wasn't all, however. He 'd also started to chew up any item of clothing that was left downstairs, much to Suzanna's distress, who was always exceptionally well dressed. Once the clothes had been placed out of reach, it didn't take long for *Truffles* to start nibbling at their expensive furniture. Hugo suspected that *Truffles* felt abandoned, being left on his own during the day and while he and Suzanna were asleep on the gallery above. At some point Hugo asked me if they could rent my storage room and deposit their furniture there. I couldn't say no. I didn't use it and besides that, it was easy money. By then he and especially Suzanna and were looking rather miserable. It was obvious that discord had crept into their relationship. Their friends rarely visited as there were only the metal bar stools to sit on. Hugo, who wasn't exactly built like a wrestler, struggled with carrying *Truffles* down and up the stairs as he was getting heavy. It was a foregone conclusion that sooner or later, *Truffles* and Hugo would have to part.

Then one evening, when I came home late, I saw Suzanna sitting on the front steps of their house. She was sobbing loudly and her whole body was shaking as she wailed. I sat next to her, handed her a tissue and put my arm around her shoulders, thinking something terrible had happened.

"Suzanna! Darling! What is wrong? What is it?" She couldn't speak immediately. She blew her nose and took some deep breaths to try and calm herself and regain her composure.

"I...." she uttered, "woohoo ...can't ...woohoo ...take it anymore." She let out another big sob and blurted out. "It's the pig...woohoo... – or me!" She spoke with a resolve and firmness in her voice. I gently squeezed her shoulder and nodded sympathetically.

"I fully understand. It is ludicrous, really."

"Yes. It is. Just think of it – to have to ask my boyfriend to choose between a pig and me. It's terrible!" She let out another loud sob and blew her nose again. She then got up rather abruptly, and made her way to the apartment where she undoubtedly issued Hugo with an ultimatum.

I didn't see either of them for a week or so and when I did bump into Hugo he told me that *Truffles* had returned to the farm he had originally come from.

"It's the best for all of us. I really liked him. I miss him" he said. "He was such a great character but I love Suzanna and I don't want to lose her. Besides, it was getting to difficult to take him out for his walks and Merlin got scared of him." Hugo sighed. "I just hope he doesn't end up as sausages on somebody's dinner plate. I couldn't bear the thought of it."

"Yes," I replied. "That's understandable."

"I'm going to visit him from time to time to see how he is doing" he mumbled before we said good-bye. We arranged a date for Hugo and Suzanna to collect their belongings from my storage room. That happened the following Saturday. They were both cheerful and Hugo made Suzanna laugh out loud by making a lot of "Oink-oink" sounds. It was obvious that domestic bliss had been restored. *Truffles* would soon become a distant memory.

STILL WATER

"Let me introduce you to Perrier," Pemma uttered as she leaned down and gingerly opened the door of the cat carrier she had placed on the floor in the hall. I knew he was a white Persian, aged 15, so quite an elderly gentleman who had lost a few of his teeth. Shyly, he poked his head out of the opening of the carrier. He sceptically inspected both me and his surroundings, and curiously sniffed my hand before retreating into the carrier, meowing quietly. "Just leave him to it," Pemma said. "He is a lovely boy and very friendly. He will come out sooner or later, to have a good look around and to eat and drink".

Pemma was off to Tibet for two months, where her father had worked for the Tibetan Government and the Tibetan Buddhist leader, His Holiness The Dalai Lama. Her family went to live in India when she was three and she moved to London in 1999. She hadn't been back since their departure and felt that the time had come to reconnect with her past and re-visit the town of Lhasa, where she had spent the first three years of her childhood. Rather than sending Perrier to a cattery where she did not believe he would get the attention he was used to, and where he would not be able to wander around freely, she had decided that I, as an animal lover, was the ideal person to take care of him.

With me in tow, Pemma went to the kitchen, laden with bags filled with various types of food for her beloved pet, who in his youth had been a prize-winning show cat and who was still very handsome indeed. Pointing at the first bag she explained, "He gets a handful of this every day in this little blue dish. It helps him to digest the fur and, as you can see, he has rather a lot of it." "Ah. I see. When do I give it to him - in the morning or in the evening?" I asked.

"Put it out in the morning, please," Pemma said. "He'll eat it throughout the day. And then you give him his wet food." She reached into a large box and dug out one of the pouches and another bowl to put it in. This was followed by a small tin that had the letters "patè" written on it, together with yet another bowl. "He knows exactly which food goes in which bowl, by the way," she insisted, "and he gets the patè in the evening."

"Alright. No problem. Why don't I open it now and empty it in his bowl?" I suggested. Pemma agreed that it was a good idea, so I duly positioned all bowls with the right food in them onto a large plastic mat in the shape of a cat's paw.

"Ah yes, and he gets one small tine of tuna fish a week also".

"Lucky cat" I commented, busy noting down her instructions and looked down on Perrier who had slinked into the kitchen, sniffing his food.

"Why don't we have a cup of tea?" Pemma proposed. "I've been so busy rushing around and could do with relaxing for a bit."

"Absolutely" was my answer. "Ginger and Lemon okay?"

"Oh lovely" she said, so I put a ginger and lemon tea bag in each of our mugs and boiled the kettle.

Meanwhile, Pemma had taken the cat litter (super clumping, as I understood, and it would last for ages) and the litter tray to the bathroom and came back to the hot steaming golden coloured ginger and lemon liquid,

As we sat on the sofa, slowly sipping our tea and talking about her forthcoming adventure, there was a "meow" by our feet. "Hello darling" Pemma said softly and patted Perrier's head. He looked a little bewildered, but seemed okay and at ease. He was not frightened of me or the unfamiliar environment and had a little wander.

"Gosh. He really is very handsome," I remarked, and then proceeded to gently stroke his long white silky coat.

"Yes, he is. It's just I've been travelling so much and he's been miserable because he knows I'm going away again. He sat on my suitcase, this morning, looking at me with his beautiful sparkling blue eyes, and refused to move. I am so glad he's with you. His eyes, by the way weep a lot and need special attention and he needs to be brushed daily, which he absolutely loves "

"The pleasure is all mine. He'll be fine" I assured her. "His being here will be good for me too."

We chatted for a bit longer, about this and that, when Pemma looked at her watch and leapt up.

"Gosh. Is that the time? I've got to be going." She leant down and picked up Perrier who looked sad as she cradled him in her arms, saying good-bye. We walked into the hall, where we hugged on her way out and I again reassured her that she needn't worry about her feline companion's welfare.

Perrier had followed me and watched me closely as I started unpacking and stowing away the different pouches and tins, when a few minutes later, the doorbell rang fiercely and unexpectedly, startling us both.

"Who could that be, old boy?" I asked him before picking up the entry phone.

It was a frantic sounding Pemma.

"Oh, Connie. There is something important I have to give you. Can you let me in please? It's rather heavy and the car is parked on a yellow line."

I pressed the entry button and she hurriedly climbed up the stairs, clutching a few large bottles of water. A little breathless, she headed straight to the kitchen and placed them on the floor. "Sorry about that."

"Well, thanks, Pemma. That is most kind" I said thinking, that they were for me.

"They are not for you," she blurted out. "I completely forgot to tell you, please don't give Perrier tap water. Not even if it's filtered." Pointing at the bottles, she then said "He only drinks Evian".

My facial expression must have been one of utter amazement and admittedly it was hard to stifle a laugh. I mean, who had ever heard of a cat named Perrier who only drank Evian? Now, that was funny and it made me chuckle for ages after she had left.

Yet, as I thought of it, it somehow made sense to me. Personally, I have a sensitive nose and don't even like the smell of tap water and with my taste buds being just as delicate, I don't like its taste either. Perhaps it was the same for Perrier?

I dutifully changed his water every day although I never actually saw him drink it. I even added a little to his food. However, Pemma had made me promise faithfully to serve only Evian. I kept my promise and we both lived happily together until her owner returned.

THE LITTLE BLACK CAR

It was nine o'clock in the morning and there was a knock at my door. My night had been restless until the small hours when I had finally fallen into a deep sleep. I tried to ignore the knocking, yet it persisted and got louder.

I couldn't imagine who might want to see me this urgently. It wouldn't be the postman. He didn't usually come till the afternoon. Then I remembered: it was my lovely elderly Italian neighbour - and now friend - Azelma who lived on the top floor but has since moved to the apartment opposite mine.

She was off to India for six weeks, where she went every year to escape the clutches of gloomy and cold English winters, and she was going to drop her car keys off.

I kicked off the duvet, put on my dressing gown and staggered to the door, still half- asleep, trying not to step on Olive, my cat, who was brushing against my legs, purring.

A quick glance at myself in the hall mirror made me sigh. "Oh gawd. I look dreadful," I muttered, and quickly ran my fingers through my hair before taking a peek through the peephole in my door to make sure it really was her. To my relief, I saw that, yes, indeed it was Azelma. I unlocked the door and slowly opened it, trying not to yawn and not to go into shock from the drop in temperature.

"Oh, hello darling," Azelma chirped as she inspected my dishevelled appearance. She herself was as well-kempt, rosy-cheeked and fresh looking, as always. "Did I wake you? I am sorry."

"No. Didn't you know that the *dishevelled look* is all the rage? Soon every woman will want to look like that, trust me. Anyway, how are you? Is it today you leave?" I asked, as I began to shiver.

She chuckled. "I feel absolutely marvellous," she replied. "Why wouldn't I be? I'm looking forward to my six weeks in Goa. The temperature is just right in February and my body and soul crave the sun. I can't stand another day of this weather. It's been getting me down."

"Yes, it's been getting me down too. It's been so dark every day – and as for the North Easterly winds? I hate them. I've hardly wanted set a foot outside unless it was absolutely necessary. Those wretched winds pretty much penetrate every layer I wear and go right into my bones. I must be getting old or something."

"Anyway, it's a beautiful day", she said, "and yes, I will be leaving in half an hour. I just wanted drop off my car keys and say good-bye." She handed me a sealed envelope. "I've written the registration number on the card as well as my daughter's phone number. If the car has to be moved because they are digging up the road yet once again, please call her. She'll come over and move it."

"Oh, of course, Azelma. I shall keep an eye on it. Where is it parked?"

With her perfectly manicured index finger, she pointed to somewhere that I took to be on the right.

"It's very close by, just over there, under the lamp post."

"Oh, that's easy enough. What make is it?"

"It's a little black Fiat *Uno*."

"No problem, Azelma," I replied, recapping her words in my mind: '*little black car parked under lamp post close to our house*'. "Consider it done."

"Oh, thank you, Darling. Is there anything you'd like me to bring you back from India?"

"Actually, yes, there is. *Vicco* toothpaste, if you can find it."

"I've not heard of it but I will look for it."

"It's a herbal toothpaste. Somebody bought it for me in India and I rather like the taste. I still haven't found a shop that stocks it. But please don't go out of your way."

"Don't worry. If I see it in a shop, I will get it."

"Anyway, I must dash. The taxi should be here soon and I prefer to get to the airport early. Good bye, dear."

"Bye, Azelma. Have a fabulous time and don't worry about your car. I shall make sure it's safe."

We waved at each other as she proceeded to ascend the stairs. I shut the door and made my way into the kitchen, still holding the envelope. I switched on the kettle, bent down to stroke Olive, who was waiting patiently for me to fill her empty bowls with her favourite food. That done, the kettle had boiled and I poured the hot water in a mug, added a squirt of fresh lemon and went to the living room.

"Gosh I am tired," I said to myself as I put the envelope in a drawer and turned on the TV to watch *Friends'*, one of my favourite programmes at the time. It always made me laugh and there is nothing better than to start the day with laughter and end it that way, too.

Three weeks had passed and as promised I had routinely checked on Azelma's little black car every other day. There had been nothing untoward until one blustery day when I was rushing to meet somebody for lunch.

As I approached the lamp post, expecting to see the car there, what greeted me was an empty space. The Fiat Punto had gone and I was in a panic. 'Oh no!' I thought. 'The car has been stolen.' I rummaged in my handbag for my mobile phone and that wasn't there either. I had left it behind.

"Blast" I uttered and ran back home, not sure what to do next. Should I inform her daughter or go straight to the police to report the theft? We still had a police station then; nowadays they are a rarity and police hold regular meetings at the local library.

I cancelled my lunch date and called Azelma's daughter. "Your mum's car has been stolen" I told her rather anxiously.

"Really? How odd. It's such an old car. Mum has had it for at least 15 years and it is not worth anything," she commented.

"I realise that. It was there yesterday and I couldn't believe my eyes when it had disappeared today. I am about to go to the police and report it."

"Maybe you don't have to report it in person," she wondered. "Perhaps it can be done over the phone?"

"I haven't a clue. I'll ring them first but I can't find the card with the details. Remind me, please, it was a Fiat Punto, right?"

"A Fiat Punto?" She sounded surprised. "No, it was a Fiat Uno."

"Yes, of course it was," I answered. "What is the registration number? "

"Sorry, I don't remember it. I have it written down but don't have it here in the office. I shall tell you it later. Don't worry too much. If the car can be found, that will be great. If not, Mum won't stress over it."

We ended the call and as I reflected on what she had said, a strange thought popped into my mind and it refused to go away. I held back telephoning the local police station, which was a good thing. Instead, I opened the drawer of the side board and took the card out of the envelope with Azelma's bold handwriting on it.

As I studied the details she had so carefully noted, I was in disbelief.

"Oh no. I am such an idiot," I whispered and sped out of the house onto the road, still clutching the card. As it turned out, I had been keeping an eye on somebody else's car for the past few weeks.

What if it actually had been stolen? My heart beat a little too fast. Then, to my relief, I spotted it – Azelma's little black car. It was still there, innocently parked under the lamp post on the *opposite* side of the street, and I could have sworn it was laughing at me.

GOING BANANAS

"It'll never catch on," I said to my friend Karen. "No, I just can't see it happen."

She gave me a questioning look across the table, took a small sip of her cappuccino and then slowly pushed the last piece of her apple strudel on to her fork and into her mouth.

It was the year 2001 and we were discussing the demise of the rather short lived *dot.com* bubble. As a result Karen had shelved her plans of starting a direct-selling business for women's clothing.

Yes, I had previously heard mentions of the Internet though only in passing and more recently from her, but my interest and understanding of modern technology was as limited as my desire to use it commercially. To sit in front of my computer and engage in buying products online was an alien concept to me. In fact, I had only very recently succumbed to getting a dial-up internet connection and an e-mail address. When I did it was only because a two of my closest friends had moved as far away as India and New Zealand and it was a great way to stay in touch. Some people I knew had mobile phones, but oh no, not me. I wasn't tempted one bit although have to admit that in some respects modern technology has somewhat simplified my life albeit I couldn't foresee it then.

"Umm. I think you are wrong." Karen replied thoughtfully. "It's true that Amazon and e-bay are struggling for survival and I have no idea how the supermarkets are doing. However, I believe online shopping will be the thing of the future."

My facial expression must have been one of blankness. The names of what must be the two largest global online retailers were meaningless to me and Karen patiently explained their function. I was amazed. As for the two leading supermarket chains who were already offering door-to-door deliveries, now that service did arouse my curiosity. Still, I was doubtful.

"No, Karen" I reiterated and shook my head. "I really can't see it taking off. I love going to the shops, having a wander around and seeing what is on offer. Doesn't everybody? Apart from grocery shopping perhaps, online shopping doesn't entice me and I dare say it wouldn't entice others. "

Famous last words they were indeed. I was not alone in assuming that online retailing would never take off, but it did. It would take more than a decade for the Internet and on-line shopping to win me over and when it did, it was purely for practical reasons.

Once a week- sometimes twice - I would shop for my elderly friend Joan, now aged 96, because she was no longer able to. I would make my way to a big supermarket by bus and guess what? I often came unprepared, forgetting that I needed to have a £ 1 coin to put in the slot for the trolley. Often I had to almost beg people to change a five pound note into coins until a kind man gave me a token so that problem was solved. And why was it that on many occasions my chosen trolley had a wonky front or back wheel and refused to go in a straight line?

Like others before me, I would quietly curse it under my breath and apologise to customers whose trolleys I bumped into. It made shopping more like an obstacle race rather than a pleasurable experience. Of course, I could have taken it back outside, hooked it up, got my £ 1 back and picked another trolley, though once inside, I wanted my expedition to end as quickly as possible. Besides, there was no guarantee that the next trolley's wheels were intact.

Apart from that, some supermarkets have the annoying habit of regularly moving products around the store. I would confidently stroll to the cooler cabinets in aisle No. 4 to buy unsalted organic butter, only to find that it now held sausages, salami and bacon.

I also frequently failed to find a member of staff to enlighten me as to the whereabouts of the butter or whatever else I hadn't been able to find. Funnily, it was usually other customers who would ably point me in the right direction when I had posed the question "Any idea where the butter lives these days?" to anyone who might happen to hear it. Some were lost, like me. "You haven't by any chance passed the aisle with the eggs?" they wanted to know.

Then there were the special offers, some of which were impossible to resist. My trolley tended to fill up quickly, with me contemplating putting some products back on their shelves. That would have added at least another twenty minutes to my trip, so I often didn't bother.

Once satisfied that I had bought everything on my list - and many items that weren't on it but would come in useful - it was a matter of looking for a till with a cashier and the shortest queue and least filled-up trolley.

Thankfully going through the *chip and pin* routine was a quick and painless exercise, unlike picking up the heavy bags and carrying them to the bus stop. My shoulders ached and the carrier bag handles had a tendency to cut into the palms of my hands. Heaving them onto the bus, there would be beads of sweat on my forehead and the journey back to my friend's flat was not something I looked forward to.

"Why did I buy so much?" I would ruefully ask myself. I vowed not to do that again and one rainy day, as I sat on the bus, which was stuck in traffic, I had one of those Eureka moments. Everyone gets them once in a while. From the depths of my mind, my conversation with Karen of ten years earlier surfaced. Hadn't she told me about being able to buy directly online from two supermarkets (both of which I frequented) and have goods delivered directly to one's home?

"I am going to have a go at this" I decided and, filled with excitement, attempted to set up an account with one of the supermarkets. Hah! It had looked easy enough but I unfortunately encountered some unexpected problems and I hadn't a clue how to solve them. That irked me. Going through the same exercise with the other supermarket, Lady Luck smiled upon me. The account was opened and I cautiously embarked on the first leg of my journey as an internet shopper. Placing Joan's first order wasn't exactly enjoyable as being a novice it had taken a lot longer than expected.

With the passage of time the ordering process took less and less time, except when the layout of the website had been changed and I hasten to add, not always in favour of its user.

It has to be said that I was and am in awe of modern technology and its creators and considered it to be infallible until one Sunday when I was forced to review not only my proficiency, but also my notion that technology *never* gets it wrong.

Joan likes fruit, especially bananas. She prefers them a little on the green side and has one every morning, neatly sliced on her peanut butter or chocolate spread sandwich or after lunch with a large dollop of whipped cream.

Her grocery order was due for delivery on the Sunday in question and I texted the carer.

"Have they been?" I wanted to know.

"Yes," she messaged back. "I am just starting to put things away and there are no substitutions."

"That's good." I replied with a sense of relief as not only had there been a problem with deliveries arriving rather late but also some strange substitutions that had to be returned. Another text followed a short while later and nothing could have prepared me for what it said.

"Why so many bananas?" it read.

"What do you mean? I ordered five. How many are there?"

A couple of minutes later she answered.

"Thirty eight."

"Thirty eight? You are joking, aren't you?"

I punched her number onto the keypad of my mobile and she picked up the call immediately. She was chuckling.

"Seriously, Mandy. Have they really delivered 38 bananas?"

"Yes. There are loads of them. The driver wanted to know if you are starting a banana bread business. "

We both laughed. It was quite funny, actually. I rarely cook and leave making banana bread to others.

"Why don't you take some home and leave a note for the other carers, telling them to help themselves? I've no idea how this happened."

I was confused. From memory, I had ordered five bananas. That is not exactly a large amount now, is it? Was it me or was cutting edge technology not quite as 'cutting edge' as we are made to believe? Since Albert Einstein wasn't around to solve this unexplained mystery, there was only one thing for me to do and that was to phone the customer services department at the supermarket.

I immediately got through to Seamus, one of the representatives, who was utterly charming and eager to help.

"Seamus," I said. "I have a bit of a problem with my delivery. I ordered five bananas and, would you believe it, we received thirty eight. Can you shed any light into how this could have happened?"

There was a moment of silence at the other end.

"Let me have a look, Mrs. Glynn. Do you have the order number?"

"Thank you, Seamus and no I don't have it to hand. I can give you the post code, if that helps."

The line went quiet again while Seamus checked my order and then gave me some unexpected news.

"You ordered five kilos of bananas".

"Five kilos? That can't be right. If you check previous orders you will find that I normally four bananas. However, on this occasion I ordered five."

"I am sorry, Mrs. Glynn. You most definitely ordered five kilos."

"Oh gosh. My mind must have been on other things and I must have moved the cursor without realising it." I then had a crucial question for him. "Tell me something. Doesn't your software have a facility that beeps and alerts the store when an unusually large order is received from a regular customer so someone can contact him or her to find out if it is correct?"

"No, I am sorry. The software isn't that advanced. The order is received and fulfilled. It is an excellent idea though and I will certainly pass it on to our IT department," Seamus said. "I tell you what else I will do. As a good will gesture and because you are a long standing customer, I shall refund you for the thirty eight bananas. "

"Oh. Thank you so much, Seamus. You are most kind. It won't happen again. Good bye"

"Good bye," he said and we both hung up.

What I learned was that a) it is important to be focussed on what I am doing so my concentration doesn't lapse and b) as *cutting edge* as modern technology is, there is still room for improvement.

Thirty three bananas went to good homes and as far as I know, none of their new owners made banana bread.

COFFEE BREAK

Tina and I had known each other for more than thirty years. We had worked at the same record export company in London and kept in contact even after we both went on to do other things. We didn't see each other regularly because Tina lived a distance away, but we had often talked about going on a little day trip together. Finally, it had happened and we were on our way to Frinton-on-sea, a rather idyllic seaside resort in Essex.

We were halfway there and had stopped at the motorway service station to stretch our legs and let Taff, her border collie, explore new territory. To my delight I'd noticed that the supermarket was one of my favourites, so was about to head there to buy myself a tea and something to nibble on, though wasn't sure what I fancied.

"Would you like me to get you a coffee while I am there?" I asked Tina. I pointed at the supermarket as she gingerly lowered her small rucksack onto the picnic bench with one hand and holding on to her dog's leash with the other.

"No thank you," Tina replied. "I brought my own."

It didn't really surprise me. She was a totally unique individual who was particular about certain things like water. She usually carried a bottle of her specially filtered and treated water with her wherever she went.

"Ok. Is there anything at all you want?"

"No, nothing, thank you," she answered.

"Alright. See you in a few minutes then."

Tina smiled. "I'll give Taff a drink and a bit of a walk in the meantime," she said.

I just nodded and visited the ladies' toilets before entering the supermarket. It was a hot day in August; the store was pleasantly cool and not very busy. The tea and coffee making facilities were right next to the doors and the shelves nearby were stocked with delicious looking sandwiches and meals to go. I picked a pasta dish, made myself a "regular" size tea in a paper cup and proceeded to the check-out. The lady who served me was friendly and chatty.

"Hot today, isn't it?" she remarked. "Would you not rather have a cold drink?" she asked, as she rung up my tea and pasta on the till.

"Yes, it is rather muggy. I tend to stick to drinking hot drinks in the heat. My grandmother insisted that it's better for the body because it's more in keeping with its temperature and I find that to be true."

"Oh. That's interesting. Personally, I want to gulp down gallons of nicely chilled drinks and then feel even hotter a few minutes later. Maybe I will try your grandma's recipe for staying cool instead."

"It does make a difference." I said. "How much do I owe you?" I enquired and once she had told me and handed me the receipt, I paid and we said good-bye.

Outside, I was hit by a gust of warm wind. Tina and Taff were still wandering around on the large grassy area with Taff sniffing here, there and everywhere and cocking his leg in just as many places. I sat at the bench, sipped my tea and watched them strolling leisurely in my direction.

Tina tied Taff's leash around the table leg and sat down.

"How's your tea?"

"It's quite nice, actually. I don't drink tea often but I had a bit of a craving today. So where's your coffee then?" I wanted to know.

"I haven't made it yet." Tina replied calmly and gingerly undid the zip of her rucksack.

Carefully she pulled out to a thermos flask, which she gently placed on the table. I looked at her and giggled.

"Tina! What are you like?"

"Actually – I don't like the taste of coffee that flows out of a little spout from a vending machine into a polystyrene or paper cup" she commented. She then very carefully pulled out something wrapped in a fluffy towel. That something turned out to be a cafetiere. This was followed by small packet of freshly ground coffee which she emptied into the cafetiere. It smelt delicious. Then she almost ceremoniously added hot water from the thermos flask and pushed the plunger down in slow motion.

While the coffee was brewing, I continued to watch Tina with amazement as she carried on taking more things out of her back pack, each one wrapped in a cloth. Next on the table appeared a white bone china cup and saucer. That was followed by a matching sugar bowl and jug which she filled with milk from a small bottle. As I later discovered, she had brought the right amount needed for three cups of coffee – no more, no less.

After a few minutes, she poured the coffee into her china cup with what could only be described as devotion, added milk, a cube of brown sugar and stirred it.

She breathed in the aroma and then took the first sip.

"There. That is my idea of a proper cup of coffee. I've packed a spare cup. Would you like to try some?"

"Wild horses couldn't make me" I joked. "But, yes please. I'd love to. It smells mouth-wateringly wonderful. So here's hoping it tastes as good as it smells."

Tina smiled and fished the spare cup and saucer out of her rucksack. She dispensed the coffee into my cup with the same devotion as with hers and put it in front of me. All it needed was a little milk and a hint of sweetness, and it was ready for consumption.

We drank our coffee in silence and enjoyed every drop. I have to admit that no cup of coffee, regardless of which Barista made it, has ever tasted even remotely similar.

Tina had done a lot more than merely add water to ground coffee followed by milk and sugar. She had added a sprinkle of love, and that had made all the difference.

L - #0187 - 131219 - C0 - 210/148/5 - PB - DID2714056